Homecoming

Hollie Bradbury

Presentation by *BookLeaf Publishing*

Web: www.bookleafpub.com

E-mail: info@bookleafpub.com

ISBN: 9789357440530

First edition 2023

To my grandparents, Eva, Jack, Marjorie and Patrick, for your part in the fond memories that make up some of this book.

ACKNOWLEDGEMENT

To the writing group' Writing for the soul' that I joined in June 2022.
I wouldn't have dared to share any of my written work if it wasn't for the supportive, encouraging space that we shared.

Thank you, Emma, for the prompts that got me thinking about what home really is and to Richard, Rachael, Lisa, Lyndsay and Pauline for listening to me while I figured it all out.

PREFACE

I was born and raised in Wakefield, West Yorkshire, and having moved to Liverpool for university, I went on to meet a fantastic scouser and never left Merseyside.

It wasn't in my plan to move away from Yorkshire permanently. The stunning Yorkshire landscape and the dulcet accent are all things I miss about the place I called home for my formative years.

As can be the case for many people in their 20s, and following the relentless lockdowns of 2020 and 2021, I struggled with my identity for a while.

Who was I? And what made me, me if I wasn't living around what was familiar and ingrained in my roots?

I finally figured this out in the Summer of 2022 when I joined a writing group. I had never been to anything like it before and didn't know what to expect.

Well, sure enough, the first prompt we were given to write about was...

'Where is home?'.

Talk about divine intervention!

And as I started scribbling down my response to that question, I realised I could always reach myself and my Yorkshire roots if I wrote about it.

During those eight weekly sessions, each prompt spurred me to delve deeper into what made me, well...me.

Not all of the poems in this book are about Yorkshire; some are reflections on what makes me who I am and the lessons I've learned along the way.

My homecoming, if you will.

I hope you enjoy my trip back home. It is my hope that if you are feeling a little lost, it helps you to get home too.

Thanks for reading!

Seaside

There's something about that shabby seaside town.

The harbour reeked of fish amidst the salty sea air.

The promenade was blessed with the hypnotic aroma of hot, sugary doughnuts pricked with the sharpness of salt and vinegar sprinkled liberally on chips.

It was the smell of freshly cut grass, the caravan door pinned open, and the sound of bacon fat spitting in the pan.

The day was always full of promise.

Rock pooling, net in hand, catch of the day.

The three of us huddled in a pop-up tent on the beach, windbreakers hunched as a storm rolled in from the North Sea.

We parked in the Kwik Save car park because it was free.

The dizzying, bright lights of the riders and the merry jingle of the 2p slot machines beckoned me inside the arcade. My eyes set firmly on the prize, a plastic keyring in the shape of a dolphin.

We rode the land train from the cliff's edge to the town centre.

I got a new pair of school shoes from the discount department store and a box of shortbread for my Nana that said 'Thanks for looking after my cat'.

The rain hammered the caravan's flat tin roof, the distant sound of a cautionary foghorn and the fleeting glow of the lighthouse beam as it circled back around.

Nice and safe today.

It's the fondest of memories in Bridlington Bay.

An ode to the pot wash

I'm 14 years old, dragging the granny trolley
down The Springs to fetch '12 bread' and '8 milk'
from Farmfoods.

It's 08:30 am, and the diner is open.

Another Saturday morning in the pot wash. My
favourite place.

Stealing the warmth from the Hobart
dishwasher. A bit of time away from the endless
shrill of Sue and the service bell.

A brilliant place to hide when a lad I like comes
in for a coffee with his family. 'Sorry, I can't talk
today. I'm in the pot wash,' I say.

My grandparents will be here in an hour, one
small, one large latte.

Lunchtime rush and my hair stinks of chip fat,
but I'll be back in the pot wash in an hour.

The intricate task of chiselling off baked-on lasagne and shortcrust pastry that's been sat on the hot plate all morning.

My walkman phone is stashed in my tabard pocket, and I check it often.

I don't work on the till or do the drinks. I told them I was allergic to coffee.

Really, I was happier in the pot wash.

A private area to devour the dregs of a braised beef pie mix oozing with gravy.

Late afternoon, I'm in the back room opening giant tins of peas in brine. Baked bean juice slops onto my tabard.

The Hat lady has thrown chips on the carpet, which have now been trodden into the pile. Albert is singing 'We'll meet again' as he cheerfully digs into his cottage pie and mash, and blind Dave needs his sausage dinner cutting up.

I observe all of this whilst folding serviettes around the boiling hot knives and forks that sit in a tub on the end of the counter.

At 4:30 pm, I'm cleaning the toilets. The
pungent aroma of watered-down bleach.

At 5 pm I'm hoovering the worn carpet with
Henry. I turn the hoover on, let it run and sit
down with my feet up out of view.

A rogue chip under a table and a runaway pea
will eventually give me away.

Depends which way you look at it

I'm missing a gang of girlfriends, six bridesmaids, and holidays to Zante in matching T-Shirts. A busy WhatsApp group, a complete history to look back on from primary school to now.

But what about the opportunity to meet new friends with different perspectives, backgrounds and experiences? The joy in someone unexpected enriching your life.

I'm missing Saturday morning, a quick cuppa in town. One small, one large latte and maybe a slice of lemon drizzle.

But what about making a real effort because you have to? The experiences and plans poured into an organised visit. An endless WhatsApp dialogue. Making the moments really count and not taking them for granted.

I'm missing A WF postcode and starting a family, knowing that a helping hand and a lasagne to reheat is only 15 minutes away.

It takes a village, after all.

But what about a helpful and capable partner who will turn his hand to anything? Always giving it a go.

Or trusting yourself that...actually, you've got this?

I'm missing not having to concern myself about the road less travelled.

But what about acknowledging that building, nurturing and growing a life away from what you know takes courage, perseverance and confidence?

And that... you're definitely not missing.

Twenties

These years are said to be so golden that one day in your twilight years, you'll look back at them with glassy eyes...or rose-tinted glasses.

I'm glad to see my 20s roll away behind me like the trackside hedgerows on an 18:48 Virgin Pendolino train to London Euston.

Goodbye, 20s. You've certainly been a ride.

A flash in the pan of finding friends, losing friends, moving cities, putting down roots, travelling to new places, messy mistakes, the highest highs, the lowest lows and everything in between.

I've dyed my hair from brown to red to blonde to blue just to find what fits.

Will this box of £5.99 permanent dye and a short edgy haircut help me to find out? If not, Topshop Joni Jeans. Dr Martens and a Zara coat will.

Heartbreak, twice, the thinnest I've ever been with bleach blonde hair and a tiny waist. The

bleeding stemmed sometimes and other times
free flowing. A pain quite unique but the
greatest teacher.

Have I stayed on track with what society says
you're supposed to do?

Says who?

Delipaitated halls of residence, feeling
homesick. Internships.
Graduation. A 2:1 with a degree I've never since
used.

Getting my first footing on the career ladder and
the hustle to move up until I decided that
working for myself was a much better option for
me.

Adopting a cat, buying a terrace house and
getting engaged.

My 20s have not welcomed parenthood. Too
scared to jump. I can hear a clock ticking louder
than ever. But where is it coming from?

Death. Grandparents - lucky we if we have them
at all. Mentors and confidants.

Wishing they'd be here for longer and feeling weird that they won't be present on my wedding day, but someone I don't like might be.

The circle of life, everyone moving up one place in the roster, including me, as I stare the next decade down the barrel.

30s, whatever you bring, I'm ready for you.

Home

Part of my home is now a compromise, but I can always get back there by writing about it.

Home is a feeling, and it can be more than one place.

Home is the city that has unexpectedly welcomed me for 11 years.

Home is where people sound like me and get a reference to 'Argos Corner'.

Home is a WF1 postcode, red WY Metro bus stops and black and white street signs written in Times New Roman font.

Home is an Edwardian Terrace House adorned with the trinkets I've collected over the years and where the cat chooses to sit on my knee.

Home is a loving embrace after a salty day.

Home is putting the fire on and cradling a mug of hot tea.

Home is wherever I want it to be.

I am…

An only child. No blueprint. Inbuilt guilt.

An observer akin to Nick Carraway. "Listen, Hollie, I know you like to watch..but don't make any judgments. We have all summer! Now, do you want to sit back and watch? Or do you want to play ball!?"

My favourite book? The Great Gatsby.

Nostalgic.

Remember it all and feel it all so deeply.

In life, you're either a dog or a cat. A playful puppy or a cantankerous cat.

I'm a cat.

Neutral skin tone, suit both gold and silver, but I want to fit into one box and know 'my colour'.

Magenta purple.

A British racing green Mini Cooper.

Yorkshire tea. Weak. The bag only in the water for a whisker of time, with lots of milk.

Emley Moor mast on the right side of the M62.

There is a light that never goes out. Happy riff. Sad lyrics.

A balance of melancholy and spirit.

I am a paradox at every angle.

Set 6 maths, Set 1 English.

Salty and Sweet.

That's me.

Nana

Lunchtime - Bob Monkhouse's Wipe Out.

A ham sandwich cut into triangles and a
mushroom cup-a-soup with croutons.

A glass of Copella apple juice and a Rolo
yoghurt is on the tray.

The same lunch every day.

Crushing dried poppy heads in our hands and
scattering the seeds around the garden.

You pushing me on my swing, soaring high
under the cherry blossom tree, its raining petals.

Watch out for Scampi!

Raking up thoughts of you..or is it me?

Beady grey eyes, perma-scowl, easily
aggravated.

Short temper, a strange way of going about
things. Independent.

Odd.

Mesmerising.

Intrinsically brunette.

Missing you every day.

Why do we take it out on our hair?

The breakup results in a mad dash to Superdrug for a box of bleach and a blonde hair dye to 'tone'.

A siren call beckoning a choppy bob when your hair is long and down past your boobs.

Of course, he left me for someone with long, flowing auburn locks.

....While I'm sat here with an irreparably damaged peroxide bob.

The hit of new hair colour, look at me, I'm somebody new, you don't know me.

Stained towels, the stink of ammonia, and the shower grout stained a muddy purple hue.

Hot roots. A yellow halo.

Jagged, broken pieces and split ends. People trying to be polite.

Dry, crispy ends toasted in a straightening iron. I can make this work.

No amount of OLAPLEX can save this now.

The power of a cup of tea

Cupping cold hands around the emanating
warmth of your favourite Cath Kidston mug.

Horrible redundancy meeting?

Cup of tea.

Blindsiding break up?

Start with a cup of tea.

The news of a loved one passing, now at peace
after a lengthy struggle.

I'll put the kettle on.

Don't know where to start?

A cup of tea will do.

Bad day at the office?

Make a brew.

The healing powers of a cup of tea, always
Yorkshire, made weak for me.

Anxiety

"Don't worry" is easier said than done when
you're programmed to feel everything so deeply.

The good, the bad, the brilliant and the ugly.

"It is a blessing to be empathetic", but even
walking down the high street feels hard seeing a
million situations emanating pain, feeling guilty
about my warm coat.

And teddy bears sat on their own on the shelf.

Or biting the head off a chocolate bunny rabbit.

Feeling out of control, and my heart pounding in
my chest.

Face burning. Hot. Panicky.

Every twinge, ache, pain, mark...straight to Dr
Google.

Health anxiety, the illness and ailments I saw as
a kid, and my Grandparents in the pits of hell.

Analysing every situation...ever.

What could go wrong?

Why haven't you thought of every scenario?

If I have time to do that, why don't you?

The pressure of making it count and trying to fit
in.

Just one day without rumination, sentimentality
and nostalgia.

Small Pleasures

Fizzy Cremant in a cut crystal flute.

A kiss on the neck with your hair lifted up.

A hot shower after exercise.

A walk on a blustery English beach.

The Autumn light that floods through the windows.

Sitting with your face in the sun, feeling the warmth tickle your cheeks.

Hot fish and chips with a side of mushy peas.

A warm body enveloping yours.

Hearing lyrics that click for the first time ever.

A particular aftershave wafting through the updraft of the underground escalator.

An unexpected cup of tea made just how you like it.

Fresh bedding, sinking into plump sheets.

The smell of geranium leave and tomato plants
marinating in a greenhouse.

A warm furry purry cat sat in a tea cosy on your
chest.

Desert Island Discs

S Club 7 - Don't Stop Moving
Eight years old. I'd never heard anything like it
before. The soundtrack of a Styltrax school
disco. The beat was like cat nip whenever it
came on the radio.

Ciara, Missy Elliot - 1,2 Step
11 years old, starting high school, cruising
dial-up internet alone. Windows XP. Eastenders
makeover game, AOL chatrooms, MSN
messenger, learning the basics of HTML via my
Piczo site pinkblushes101. Black Bench jacket
with thumb holes.

Sia & Flo Rida - Wild Ones
Seventeen years old. A fake ID. A packet of
menthols to use as a prop in the smoking area.
Stumbling down the cobbled back streets in a
pair of wedges. Nights on the terrace, chatting
up an older guy to get a wristband to enter the
club. A bottle of WKD.

The Rolling Stones - Gimme Shelter
Eighteen years old. Moving away to university.
Hating every minute of it but was too paralysed

and full of pride to quit. The first one in the
family to go to uni, after all. Playing this loudly
through my earphones as I unlocked the front
door to the flat share of hell.

M83 - Midnight City
Twenty years old. Bright lights, big city, chasing
a media career in London. A failing
long-distance relationship finally led to an SW1
postcode, a Summer of love.
A Holly leaf tattoo, I've finally made it.

George Michael - Fastlove
Mid-twenties. Pleasurably living alone in a
bedsit I called an apartment. My island. Desk
positioned under a sash window, Carrie
Bradshaw style. Climbing up the career ladder,
driving around in my Peugeot 107, Keith.
Dating, heartbreak, dating, heartbreak, finding
my partner in front of a microwave emanating
an unholy stench. Where would I be now if I
hadn't pulled that out and put my soup in?

The Smiths - There is a light that never goes out
Every age. An anthem.

Quotes to live by

I have no idea who thought of these statements.

If it was you, thank you.

I have them on post-it notes littered around my desk, written in my diary and scribbled into my memory.

For the times when you don't know if you should...

"There is nothing to lose and everything to gain".

For the times when you want change to happen...

"You have to make space for good things to happen."

For the times when you need to see change...

"Take back control of things that don't make you happy."

For the times you wonder if you're neurotic...

"I demand a lot of others because I demand a lot
of myself."

For the times when you need to see the
positives, even if you are a raging pessimist...

"Life is sometimes sad and often dull, but there
are currants in the cake".

For the times when you feel regretful...

"There are no right decisions, just decisions you
make right".

For when you feel things will never improve...

"It is the things that we can't control that end up
changing us."

5 years from now...

I'll be 33 years old.

I cried when I turned 28 because I felt I needed to make big choices about having children.

I cried at the lack of time left to travel and see new places.

Maybe when I'm 33 years old, I'll be a mum? Will I do a good job?

Maybe when I'm 33 years old, I'll be married? A party for who?

Maybe my copywriting business is still going. Maybe someone is helping me?

Maybe my hair will be longer, more feminine, and make my face look thinner. Maybe it'll be that perfect tone of honey brown.

Maybe my car will be paid off.

Will my Grandma still be alive? And if she is, what state is she in?

Who will I be 5 years from now...

Energy Givers

Picking blackberries from the bushes adorning
the country lanes in late August.

Paddling in fresh, cold water.

Decluttering your space.

Noise-cancelling headphones and your favourite
song turned up loud.

A 3-hour conversation that feels like 3 minutes
with the right person.

A bright, cheery lipstick in a punchy pink.

The cat sat in a tea cosy on a fluffy rug by the
fire.

A steaming bowl of garlicky tomato pasta
covered in cheese.

Sinking in a book that you feel was written
about you.

People I admire

People who thrive on and enjoy large group activities and planned fun.

People who love watching films.

People who are unphased by the unknown.

People who don't observe and just be/are.

People who notice the smallest details.

People with a natural curiosity.

People with emotional intelligence.

People radiating kindness.

People who are reliable.

People with self-discipline.

Let go

Let go of other people's expectations.

Let go of guilt.

Let go of the roadmap provided by somebody who has never walked a day in your shoes.

Let go of beauty standards.

Let go of people's options of whom you'd never ask advice.

Let go of how you think it should be.

Homecoming

I've been transported to places I look upon
fondly like an old friend.

The salty sea air of that shabby seaside town.

Taking a notepad around the caravan park and
auditing each make and model, how many of
each and in which colourway.

This would be my specialist subject on
Mastermind.

A lunchtime nap, being roused by the tinny
jingle of 'If you go down to the woods today'.

Saturday lunchtime, Radio 2 news jingle, going
downtown.

A department store cafe. 2 lattes. Feeling grown
up with a tall spoon and glass mug. We're
positioned perfectly, a great vantage point to see
the floppy-haired sixth former working in TK
Maxx.

Another morning in the pot wash. Scraping off crusted-on lasagne and braised beef pie that's been sat on the hot plate for 5 hours.

Stacking little bottles of Britvic Orange in the fridge under the bar. Sticky dance floor, the pungent smell of stale cigs and watered-down bleach. Going to work with Dad.

By writing for the soul, I've confronted a primary source of heartburn head-on.

Home is now a compromise, but I can get back there by writing about it.

I am…

An only child.

An observer.

Cat person.

I remember it all and feel it all so deeply.

Yorkshire tea.

Artificial reddish brown hair, square-shaped face, a size 14 to see.

Writing for the soul has peeled back what it means to be me.

www.ingramcontent.com/pod-product-compliance
Lightning Source LLC
La Vergne TN
LVHW010921200726
843509LV00013B/2018